DOG BIRTH

CAKES

COOKBOOK

Healthy Dog Cakes And Treats Recipes With Frosting, Icing And Toppings Suitable For Your Dog's Adoption Day Anniversary Birthday Party Celebration And Special Occasions. (Over 35 Recipes)

Scott Thelton

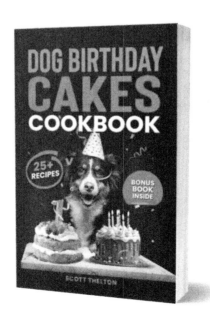

GET ACCESS
TO MORE AND
FUTURE BOOKS
BY ME

TABLE OF CONTENT

ABBREVIATIONS

cup	cup	**tablespoon**	tbsp
pound	Ib	**tablespoons**	tbsps
pounds	lbs	**quart**	qt
ounce	oz	**not available**	N/A
ounces	ozs	**minute**	min
package	pkg	**minutes**	mins
pint	pt	**hour**	hr
teaspoon	tsp	**hours**	hrs
teaspoons	tsps	**and**	&

Owning a dogs bring boundless joy, as they are source of unconditional love and never-ending frolic for the owners. As a dog parent, it's your responsibility to take care of your fur baby in every way possible. **Celebrating your pup's birthday** is a chance to show them how much you care, providing you the opportunity to infuse creativity into decorations, games, toys, and homemade treats, creating a memorable day for your beloved canine!

My dear cousin **Ivyann**, loved celebrating every little thing, including her furry friend's birthday. A cheerful young woman who adopted **Bailey** from the local shelter half a decade ago, marking the beginning of a lifelong friendship. Ivyann consistently reciprocates the love and companionship she received from her pup, from scouring the local pet store for the perfect **birthday toys and gifts**, to baking pupcakes and **special dog treats** and organizing grand parties with dog-friendly decorations for Bailey & Friends every year.

She never misses a chance to return all the favors she got from her loyal companion. That is why Bailey's birthday and adoption day had become an annual celebration. Featured in the **"DOG BIRTHDAY CAKES COOKBOOK"** are his delightful recipes, perfectly made for pet owners like you, seeking top-tier homemade pupcakes, beefcakes, pancakes, cupcakes and all kinds of healthy dog-friendly cakes for their canine companion.

It unfolds over *35 Easy DIY Homemade Dog Cakes Recipes to Celebrate Your Dog's Birthday, Adoption Anniversary, Training Graduation Day and Special Occasions.*

Imagine baking **Molasses Ginger BreadCake**, **Bacon Butter Pumpkin Pupcakes, and Strawberries Crepe Cake** to no-bake recipe **like Pancakes Tofu Frosting, to** gain-free **Zucchini BeanCake, to** frozen **Berry Raw MeatCake, Beef Cheese & Potato Pie**, **Sun Butter Carrot Cake,** and an array of other sweet and tasty creations. You'll find an array of recipe that are easy-to-follow, budget-friendly.

I wouldn't want to tell you how tasty these cakes are, but if you can trust **Bailey's judgment**, these recipes are all super delicious. Though some of them requires a little bit of patience, they are all easy & affordable options, and they are also perfect for training a puppy or rewarding your fur baby.

Now, it's your turn to add a flavorful touch to **your pet's birthday and special occasions experience** with the recipes in this cookbook, your pooch will thank you with endless tail-wagging joy.

Celebrating your pup's birthday is a great way to show them how much you care and also creates lasting memories for both of you. *Here's ten (10) great reasons why you should celebrate your dog's birthday and even throw a party for them every year;*

Special Treats & Cake:

Who doesn't love birthday cake? One of the best parts of celebrating your dog's birthday is through specialised treats. There are lots of dog bakeries producing pupcakes, cupcakes and occasional sweets, but if you know how to bake a beautiful multi-layered birthday cake for your furry friend. When you create special treats for your pup's birthday, you get to focus on high-quality, nutritious and dog-safe ingredients. This homemade approach not only supports your dog's digestive health, but also reinforces positive eating habits, and even promotes dental health.

They are Big Part of The Family:

Ivyann, my dear cousin, has had dogs her entire life, and she can't imagine her home without Barley, her loyal companion. He snuggles next to her whenever she's cold; he's patient enough to wait every day for her to walk through the door when she gets home. Bailey is always on Ivyann's side, either walking, playing, protecting or guarding her against evil and accidents. Is it any wonder that Dog spelled backwards is God? Birthdays only come once a year, the best you can do for your four-legged companion is to treat them to something special knowing they are members of your family, and also a big part of your life.

Show Love & Appreciate Them:
Not only is celebrating your dog's birthday a great way to express your love and appreciation for them, but also a fun way to celebrate their life and make them feel truly special. Of Course they bring us so much joy and happiness, it's only natural that we want to return the favor. In fact, celebrating your dog's birthdays is your way of showing gratitude for living their lives to always be with you. Thank them for the unconditional love and affection they offer you, with a new toy or a special treats and a pupcake.

Celebrate Their Health & Milestones:
A milestone birthday might feel unnecessary, but, significantly, your puppy has come a long way. Just like humans, dogs go through different life stages, and each birthday marks a milestone. Celebrating your pup's birthday is a way to embrace these stages of their life, and also an opportunity for you to reflect on their health journey from the energetic puppy years to the more laid-back senior moments. Infact it's a chance to appreciate their growth and ensure they've been receiving optimal canine nutrition, contributing to their overall well-being.

Your Furry Friend Deserves A Party:
What better way to show them how much they mean to us than by throwing them a birthday party? It'll be a day they'll never forget. Being your best friend, your dog deserves to get

a birthday party celebration with pupcakes and some memorable moments.

I couldn't wait to decorate, sing happy birthday, shower her with presents and treats, and savor a sweet slice of cake.

Bond Strengthening:

Your pup's birthday celebration provides a unique moment to reinforce the bond between you and your furry friend. Sharing birthday cake, playful activities or even a special dog treats can deepen the connection you both have, foster a positive, stronger and more meaningful relationship. At the end enhancing the emotional well-being of your beloved canine companion.

Encourage Socialization:

When you celebrate your dog's birthday, either with a playdate or by inviting friends and family who bring along their four-legged companions for a backyard gathering. This not only allows for a fun time but also improves your dog's socialization skills, positively impacts their behavior and temperament, and contributes to their overall well-being. It gets to break down any feelings of isolation or social anxiety through the joy of shared play.

Dog's Playdate:

Another compelling reason to celebrate your dog's birthday is to use the day as perfect excuse to host a playdate with some friend's and family's dog. Have them bring over their four-legged friends to celebrate and socialize in your backyard! It is imperative for your dog to become socialized so they can lead a healthy, non-stressful life. Utilizing the birthday party as a reason for letting all the dogs play together in a group setting can help alleviate feelings of isolation or social anxiety.

Snap Cute Photos & Video Memories:
You probably already have tons of pictures with your dog. However, having individual images with your dog, their dog friends, and their owners (your friends too), are unique images and precious moments you would want to last long. You get to embrace the opportunity to be the proud "dog mom or dad" and share the joy with a plethora of photos. It's a moment to capture the essence of the celebration and proudly proclaim that it's your dog's extraordinary day.

Flaunt Your Dog On The Gram:
Sharing your dog's specialized homemade treats and showing off their birthday pictures on social media platforms like Instagram can be a beautiful way to connect with fellow pet lovers; you get to inspire and even educate them about the benefits of home-cooked dog treats. This is a fun way to express your creativity and also tell your fans & followers that it's your pup's birthday, and get to prove to them that you love your dog more.

Before you start baking and making your own homemade dog cakes & treats recipes, here are a few tips to consider;

Vet-Approval:

Always consult with your vet before introducing a new recipe to your dog. Be mindful of food allergies your pet may have to specific ingredients and avoid them. If you are unsure about a specific ingredient found here, introduce the treats or food to your pets in small amounts first. You should already know that treats are not meant to replace a full balanced meal or diet for your dog.

Serving Size:

Serving sizes for these recipes can vary depending on your dog's breed, weight, activity levels, specific dietary requirements, as well as size of ingredients, desired shapes and cookie cutters used. You might want to consult with your vet to determine the appropriate serving size for your dog.

Storage:

Homemade dog treats do not contain preservatives, so it's important you store them properly to avoid spoil. Keep dried treats in glass jars, airtight container containers, or plastic food-storage or ziplock bags in in a cool, dark, dry area or refrigerator for a week, or freeze any treats your dog won't eat within a week to maintain freshness.

Toxic Ingredients:

Avoid using ingredients that are toxic to dogs such as onions, grapes, raisins, chocolates etc. Also make sure you are using only all-natural peanut butter which does NOT contain artificial sweetener like xylitol as an ingredient. Your chicken bone broth should be the option that has no sodium, no onion or garlic. Same with other ingredients.

Invest in Silicone Baking Cups: Silicone baking cups make it super easy to pop your dog treats and cupcakes out. They also help keep your treats from breaking when removing them from the cups.

35+ DOG-FRIENDLY CAKE & TREATS RECIPES

As you flip the next page, you're going to explore over 35 Dog Cakes & Treats Recipes, put together to delight your pooch on their *Birthday, Adoption Anniversary, Training Graduation Day, Valentine's Day, Love Your Pet Day, Special Occasions & All Year Round.*

1. Whole-Wheat Pupcakes

Ingredients:
- 2 cups whole wheat flour
- 2 cups rolled oats
- 1½ cups carrot purée
- 1½ cups coconut milk
- ½ cup peanut butter
- 3 tbsps cornstarch
- water (adjust as needed)

Instructions:
To start, preheat oven to 390°F (200°C)
In a mixing bowl, combine flour & oats. Mix carrot purée. Prepare batter with as much water as needed. Lightly grease a cake pan and pour batter into it.
If desired, decorate cake surface with dog food and treats.
Place into oven and bake for about 45 mins. Once cake is done, set it aside to cool at room temperature.

For The Frosting
In a mixing bowl, combine peanut butter & coconut milk. Add in cornstarch dissolved in some water and blend at a fast speed. Apply the layers of frosting on it. Lastly, top the cake with the dog biscuits.

Tips/Notes:
If coconut milk is unavailable, you can use plain yogurt as a substitute. Keep in mind that frosting mixture doesn't get too warm, you can simply place the mixing bowl on ice cubes to keep it a bit cool - then refrigerator for some minutes.

Ingredients:

- ½ cup blackstrap molasses
- ¾ cup tapioca flour
- ⅓ cup coconut flour
- ⅛ cup coconut oil (melted)
- 1½ tsp cinnamon
- 1½ tsps baking powder
- 2 tsps ground ginger
- 3 to 4 whole eggs
- coconut (finely shredded)

Instructions:

To start, preheat oven to 350°F (180°C).

In a bowl, combine all ingredients together. Stir until well combined. Fill each muffin cup with over ⅓ cup of mixture. Bake for about 25 to 35 mins, or until a toothpick inserted comes out clean.

Allow pupcakes to cool completely.

If you desire decoration, use a pastry brush to apply a thin layer of molasses over part of the pupcake. Dust with shredded coconut.

Tips/Notes:

You might end up needing some extra molasses but it's totally optional.

You can use regular muffin tin or stocking pans, be sure it's silicone.

You can use maple syrup as an alternative to blackstrap molasses.

Ingredients:

- 1¾ cups all-purpose flour
- 1 cup almond milk (not regular)
- ½ cup canned pumpkin
- ½ cup maple syrup
- ¼ cup coconut oil (melted & cooled)
- ½ tsp cinnamon
- ½ tsp baking powder
- 1 tsp baking soda
- 1 tsp apple cider vinegar
- 1 tsp salt (optional)

Frosting;

- ⅔ cup plain greek yogurt (or dairy-free)
- ¼ cup maple syrup

Instructions:

To start, preheat oven to 350°F (175°C). Lightly grease cake pans with coconut oil and line with parchment rounds; set aside. In a bowl, add flour, baking powder, baking soda, cinnamon & pinch of salt (if using). Mix until well combined.

In a separate bowl, combine pumpkin, milk, maple syrup & vinegar until well mixed.

Combine dry ingredients into wet ingredients mixture, and add in melted coconut oil. Thoroughly mix with a rubber spatula or hand mixer until well done.

Pour batter into prepared cake pans, tapping the pan on the counter a few times to even out batter.

Place pans into oven and bake for about 30 mins to 1hrs, or until cake inside dries out and a toothpick inserted into center comes out clean.

Once done, allow to cool completely before frosting.

For Frosting

Mix together yogurt & maple syrup. Once cake is cooled down, use a serrated knife to level the cake tops (cut off unnecessary cake pieces). Ice or cover it with yogurt-syrup frosting. Then serve.

Tips/Notes:

Consider adding a drizzle of peanut butter, cheese or brussels sprouts, chopped nuts or shredded coconut on top cake for an extra treat your dog will definitely love.

Using 4-inch (instead of 6-inch) cake pans is easier to place on top of baking sheet so they don't accidentally spill.

You can adjust sweetness of frosting by adding more or less maple syrup according to your taste preferences.

If desired, you can make the recipe into cupcakes without frosting, and it will still be a hit

Ingredients:
- 1 cup fresh zucchini (finely shredded)
- 2 whole eggs
- ½ tsp oregano
- ½ tsp basil
- 1 tsp olive oil
- 1 cup chicken stock (or water)
- 1¼ cup tapioca flour
- 1¼ cup garbanzo bean flour:
- 1 tbsp sundried tomato (optional)
- 1 tbsp feta cheese crumbles (optional)

Instructions:
To start, preheat oven to 350°F (180°C).

In a bowl, beat together eggs, zucchini & herbs. Stir in chicken stock (or water if using). Gradually add in flour little at a time, stirring to form a batter. If desired, stir in sundried tomato pieces or feta cheese to add extra flavors.

Gently fill silicon mini muffin cups half full of batter (you shouldn't be tempted to overfill it). Place into oven, back for about 20 to 25 mins, or until a toothpick inserted comes out clean. Allow to completely cool before removing from the molds.

Tips/Notes:
If using chicken stocks, be sure it's onion-free otherwise use water. You can use chickpea flour instead of garbanzo bean flour. Be aware that warm pupcakes will try to break or decide to stick if you try to force it out too soon.

5. Frozen Banana Butter Yogurt

Ingredients:
- 2 medium bananas (chopped & frozen)
- ¼ cup natural peanut butter
- ¾ cup plain greek yogurt
- 1 tsp honey (or maple syrup)
- ¼ cup almond milk
- banana slices for garnish

Toppings
- whipped cream
- sprinkles (just a few for color)
- dog treats
- freshly sliced bananas

Instructions:

Slice bananas into 1 inch slices. Layer onto a baking sheet and freeze banana for about 2 hrs, or until frozen solid. Line a loaf pan with a piece of parchment paper. Remove bananas from freezer and reserve some chunks for topping.

In a blender or food processor, add frozen banana slices, peanut butter, greek yogurt & honey. Blend for a few minutes. Gradually add in almond milk, continue to blend until smooth.

Once done, pour onto the prepared loaf pan, then add the reserved banana slices on top. Cover with plastic wrap and freeze for about 10 to 12 hrs, or overnight until frozen yogurt hardens. Serve with dog-friendly toppings.

Tips/Notes:

Ensure that the dog treats used as toppings are safe and suitable for your dog's consumption.

Ingredients:
- 1¼ cup whole wheat flour
- 1¼ cup carrots (processed)
- ½ cup natural sun butter
- ¼ cup canola (or veggies oil)
- 1 tsp baking soda
- 1 large egg
- 2½ tbsps honey (or maple syrup)
- 1 tsp pure vanilla extract

Frosting:
- ½ cup plain greek yogurt
- ½ cup natural sun butter
- optional dog treats (for garnishing)

Instructions:

To start, preheat oven to 350°F (175°C). Lightly grease a 6-inch round cake pan, then set aside.

In a medium bowl, whisk together egg, sun butter (or pumpkin purée or mashed potatoes), vanilla extract, oil & honey (or maple syrup).

In another bowl, stir together flour & baking soda. Add dry mixture to wet ingredients mixture bowl, mix until well combined. Gently fold in carrots until batter is thick.

Transfer batter to prepared pan, spreading it flat. Place in oven and bake for about 30 mins, or until edges start to pull away from pan. Once done, allow to cool before removing from pan.

For the Frosting

Using a hand mixer, whip sun butter with yogurt until smooth. Once cake is completely cooled, frost as desired. Decorate with any dog treats or with small amount of dog-friendly sprinkles.

Tips/Notes:

You can substitute sun butter with approximately ⅔ cup pumpkin puree or plain mashed potatoes if desired.

If using pumpkin puree, stir it over medium heat until it reduces and thickens.

This recipe yields one 6-inch cake, and if you intend to serve as treats, it should be cut into small slices in addition to your pup's regular meals.

Ingredients:
- 1 cup whole wheat flour (or coconut)
- 2 whole eggs (beaten)
- ½ cup coconut milk (unsweetened)
- ½ cup cream cheese (whipped)
- 1 cup strawberries (sliced)
- ½ cup water

Instructions:
In a bowl, combine flour, water, coconut milk & eggs. Whisk together until a smooth batter forms.

Heat a non-stick skillet on a stovetop. Ladle approximately ¼ cup of batter into the center of pan. Tilt or swirl pan to ensure an even coating on the base. Once edges start lifting, use a spatula to gently release away edges, then toss pan to flip crepe. Cook until both sides turn a light golden color.

Repeat with all remaining batter. Use a 3-inch circular cookie cutter to cut out two pieces from each crepe.

On a plate, place one piece of cut out crepe, then spread a thin layer of whipped cream cheese; add a layer of chopped fruit. Repeat this process, until you finish with a crepe on top (let the final layer be a crepe).

Once done, gently press down to secure layers. Ice entire pupcakes with a thin layer of whipped cream cheese.

Top cake with an additional fruit, then serve!

Tips/Notes:
Hot crepes can melt ingredients really quickly, allow your crepes to cool before filling them.

This recipe is perfect for your dog's breakfast and it yields about 1 crepe cake.

Ingredients:
- 1 lb ground turkey
- ¼ cup oats
- ¼ cup cheddar cheese
- ¼ cup applesauce (unsweetened)
- 1 large egg
- 1 cup natural peanut butter
- 1 tbsp vanilla extract

Instructions:
To start preheat oven at 350°F (175°C).
In a medium bowl, combine turkey, eggs, cheese & oats, until it forms a well-incorporated meatloaf dough. Place mixture in a greased pan. Then bake for about 35 mins, or until fully cooked. Allow meatloaves to completely cool down, then level it by removing the top using a knife or leveler.

For the Icing;
In a bowl, mix together peanut butter, applesauce & vanilla extract. Ice meatloaf cake with icing mixture. Serve to your dog!

Tips/Notes:
Feel free to experiment with other decorative icing as well using prepared peanut butter icing or any dog-friendly alternatives.
You can enhance the aesthetic appeal by sprinkling on some coconut shavings.
This cake recipe's serving size yields about 1 mini cake.

Ingredients:
- 1 cup oats (pulsed)
- 1 ripe banana (mashed)
- 1 tbsp ground flax seeds
- ½ cup unsweetened plant milk
- fruits (for decorating)

Frosting
- ½ cup white beans
- 3½ ozs smoked tofu
- 1½ tbsps tahini (or seed butters)
- 1 tsp turmeric
- ⅓ cup unsweetened plant milk (or water)

Instructions:
In a food processor or blender, add oats. Pulse until oat flour forms. Add in banana, ½ cup milk & flax seeds, blend until it forms a smooth pancake batter. Heat a nonstick pan over medium heat (or lightly grease your pan with coconut oil, if yours isn't nonstick). Using a small spoon or ladle, add batter to hot pan, then cook for about 2 mins on both sides. Once done, allow to cool completely, then frost.

To Prepare Frosting.
In a blender or food processor, add tofu, beans, tahini & turmeric. Process for a few minute(s). Gradually add in ⅓ cup milk or water (if using), until it reaches a thick hummus-like consistency.

To Assemble Cake
In a bowl or plate, put a dab of tofu cream. Place pancake on top, and spread some tofu cream on the pancake, then add the second pancake. Repeat with remaining pancakes until finish. Be sure all ingredients are cold, so things won't melt together.

Frost sides of the cakes with rest of the tofu cream. If desired, smooth out the frosting for a polished look. Decorate cake with a dog-safe treats. Serve to your dog and their friends.

Tips/Notes:
Your fruits/veggies can include cucumber, coconut, carrot, bell pepper, etc. You can even use mashed pumpkin or sweet potato in place of bananas for this pancake.

You can try other dog-safe coloring for frosting like spirulina, beet powder or berry powders; and can also add all decorations on top cake, or you hide some between the layers.

You will end up with about 4 to 5 small pancakes, and you can cool them faster inside fridge before frosting.

When assembling cake, don't use more than 5 small pancakes for a single cake to avoid collapsing.

Ingredients:
- 2 cups oat flour
- 2 overripe bananas (mashed)
- 3 medium carrots (shredded)
- 2 tbsps honey
- ¾ tsp baking soda
- ½ cup coconut milk (unsweetened)

Instructions:
To start, preheat oven to 350°F (175°C).

In a bowl, mix oat flour and baking soda. In a separate bowl, combine coconut milk, honey, mashed bananas & ½ a cup of shredded carrot. Whisk wet ingredients into the dry ingredients to make cake batter. Grease a cupcake tray with cooking spray or butter. Scoop batter into each cup until ¾ full. Place in oven and bake cupcakes for about 30 mins, or until a toothpick stuck into cakes comes out clean & dry. Once baked, allow to completely cool.

Frosting (Optional):

Puree remaining amount of shredded carrots to form a carrot paste icing. Frost pupcakes with carrot paste icing, and top with additional carrot shreds. Serve to your dog.

Tips/Notes:
Shred about ½ a cup of carrots for the batter and reserve an additional 1 cup for the optional frosting.

Alternatively, you can use a limited quantity of cream cheese as frosting instead of carrot shreds.

You can also use molasses as a natural sweetener instead of honey, but ensure it's in moderation.

Ingredients:
- ½ lb ground beef
- 2 medium russet potatoes
- 2 tbsps milk
- ¼ cup carrot (shredded)
- ⅓ cup quick-cooking rolled oats
- ¼ cup fresh parsley (chopped)
- 1 large egg
- 4 cups water

Instructions:

To start, preheat oven to 350°F (175°C).

In a bowl, mix egg with parsley, add meat, carrot, & oats. Continue to mix until well combined. Pour mixture into a 1-cup ovenproof baking dish. Place into oven and bake for about 45 mins. Remove from oven and allow to cool.

While the beefcake is cooling, bring water to a boil, then add in potatoes. Decrease heat to medium and cook for about 15 mins, or until potatoes are pierceable with a knife. Once done, drain and allow to cool for about 10 mins. Add milk and mash with a potato masher or handheld mixer for about 2 mins, or until smooth (be careful not to overmix, to avoid potatoes been gummy). Remove cake from pan and place on a plate. Frost cake with potato mixture. Serve your dog.

Tips/Notes:

Avoid using calorie-dense cream cheese and sugar often found in pet frostings. If preferred, you can switch beef with turkey or chicken meat if preferred.

Your potatoes should be cleaned of eyes and green spots, then peeled and chopped into quarter.

Ingredients:

- 1 cup unbleached flour
- 1 tsp baking soda
- 3 tbsps bacon fat
- ½ cup pumpkin puree (unsweetened)
- ½ cup applesauce (unsweetened)
- ¼ cup natural peanut butter
- 2 tbsps organic honey
- 2 whole eggs

For Frosting:

- ½ cup plain greek yogurt
- ¼ cup natural peanut butter
- 3 to 4 slices smoked bacon

Instructions:

To start, preheat oven to 350 F (175°C). Grease an 8 inch round baking pan and line with parchment paper.

Pan fry thick slices of bacon until crisp. Set the bacon aside and reserve the bacon fat.

In a large bowl, add bacon fat, peanut butter, pumpkin puree, applesauce & honey. Whisk until well combined. Whisk in eggs. Gradually stir in flour & baking soda until the batter is well combined. Pour batter into prepared pan and bake for about 25 to 30 mins, or until a knife inserted in center comes out clean. Set aside to cool.

<u>For Frosting</u>

In a bowl, stir yogurt & peanut butter together until smooth. Once cake is completely cool, slice it in half through the middle. Fill cake with half the frosting, then top with the rest. Decorate cake with cooked bacon. Serve to your dog.

Tips/Notes:

If you have leftovers, just crumble it to make bite-sized cake balls, then store in freezer and defrosted as treats when needed.

You should use only plain greek yogurt, as regular yogurt may make the frosting too runny.

You can use two small heart-shaped pans instead of an 8-inch round for a special occasion treats.

Ingredients:
- 1 cup whole wheat flour
- 1 cup natural peanut butter
- 1 tbsp olive oil
- 2 large eggs
- ⅔ cup plain yogurt

For Frosting
- ½ cup creamy peanut butter
- ½ cup whole wheat flour

Instructions:
In a large bowl, combine peanut butter, eggs, yogurt & oil. Mix together with a hand mixer until fully blended. Add in flour, continue to mix until well combined.

Line silicone cupcake liners with paper liners (if desired) or cook in the silicone. Place them on the air fryer tray without overlapping. Divide cupcake mixture evenly between liners.

Place tray inside and cook at 325°F (163°C) for about 12 to 15 mins. Once done, remove from air fryer and allow to cool completely before frosting (or serve to your dog as a muffin).

For The Frosting
In a bowl, combine peanut butter & flour together. Mix until smooth & creamy. Put mixture into a pastry or ziplock bag with one corner tip cut off. Then frost pupcakes.

Tips/Notes:
If desired, sprinkle a few liver sprinkles over the top before serving. Remember to store treats to retain freshness.

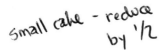

small cake - reduce by ½

Ingredients:

- 2 cups coconut flour
- 2 whole eggs
- 2 tbsps honey
- 2½ tbsps coconut oil (melted)
- ¼ cup blueberries

Frosting

- 2 tbsps honey
- ¾ cup plain yogurt
- blueberries & strawberries (for topping)
- natural food coloring

Instructions:

To start, preheat your oven to 350°F (175°C).

In a bowl, mix together eggs, honey & melted oil. Stir in coconut flour & blueberries. Lightly grease a 4-inch spring form pan with some coconut oil. Fill up pan with batter. Place into oven and bake for 25 to 30 mins, or until center is firm. Allow to cool before frosting (if desired).

For Frosting

Mix together honey, yogurt & food coloring for cake topping. Cover cake with frosting, then decorate with strawberries & blueberries.

Tips/Notes:

You can get creative with the toppings by arranging them in any shape of your choice (around edges, or create your dog's age in numbers or a message in the center).

For an egg-free option, try using about ¼ cup of unsweetened applesauce or mashed bananas per egg.

15. Liver Honey CornCake

Ingredients:
- ½ cup freeze-dried liver
- ¼ cup organic honey
- ½ cup cornmeal
- ½ cup unbleached white flour
- 1 cup whole wheat flour
- 1 tsp baking soda
- 1 tsp baking powder
- 1 tsp molasses
- 1 large egg
- 1 cup water

Frosting
- 7 to 8 ozs low-fat cream cheese (softened)
- 2 tbsps organic honey
- ⅓ cup vegetable oil

Decoration (optional)
- 3 to 4 ozs low-fat cream cheese (softened)
- ¼ cup vegetable oil
- ¼ cup carob powder

Instructions:

To start, preheat oven to 350°F (175°C). In a blender, put liver and blend into a powder. In a large bowl, combine the rest of cake ingredients until a smooth batter forms.

Pour batter into a greased and floured 8-by 8-by 2-inch baking pan. Place pan into oven and bake for about 25 mins, or until cake is completely cooked and a toothpick inserted in the center comes out clean.

Allow the cake to cool completely on a wire rack. Once cooled, prepare the frosting.

To prepare frosting:

In a bowl, mix cream cheese, honey & oil until smooth. Spread a thin layer of frosting over cooled cake. In a separate bowl, mix ingredients for decorative frosting until smooth. Place mixture in a piping bag, frost and decorate cake as desired.

Tips/Notes:

If desired; before frosting, make a stencil in shape of a dog bone, place it on top cake, and then cut cake to shape.

You can experiment with other dog-friendly flavors like pumpkin or sweet potato in the frosting.

Remember to store leftovers in the refrigerator; just bring cake to room temperature before serving again.

Ingredients:
- 2 cups oat flour
- 2 whole eggs
- ¾ cup pumpkin puree
- ½ cup applesauce (unsweetened)
- ¼ cup natural peanut butter
- 1½ tsp baking soda
- ½ tsp baking powder
- ½ tsp cinnamon

Frosting
- 1 cup plain yogurt
- ½ cup natural peanut butter
- dog treats (for garnishing)

Instructions:
To start, preheat oven to 350°F (175°C). Grease and flour two 6-inch round cake pans. Set aside.

In a medium bowl, add oat flour, baking soda, baking powder & cinnamon. Whisk to combine. Gently fold in pumpkin puree, applesauce, eggs & peanut butter. Whisk again until well combined. Add in flour, mix with a wooden spoon until a smooth batter forms.

Evenly divide batter between two prepared pans. Place into oven and bake for about 30 to 35 mins, or until a toothpick inserted comes out clean. Allow cakes to cool in pan for about 8 to 10 mins, before transferring them to wire rack to cool completely.

Using a cake leveler or knife, trim off top of one of the cakes. Spread a thin layer of yogurt on top of trimmed layer, then place the other layer on top.

In a small bowl, mix remaining yogurt & peanut butter until well combined. Use a small spatula to frost a thin layer around entire cake. Garnish with extra peanut butter, or even some dog treats.

For The Frosting:
In a bowl, mix greek yogurt & peanut butter until well combined. Spread over cake. Store in refrigerator until ready to serve.

Tips/Notes:
Be sure to use only unsweetened creamy natural peanut butter. This dog treat is also human-grade, so feel free to indulge along with your furry friend.
If your dog is sensitive to pumpkin, try this recipe with sweet potato puree as it can be a tasty alternative.

Ingredients:

- 1 cup whole wheat or white flour
- ¼ cup natural peanut butter
- ¼ cup vegetable (or canola oil)
- ⅓ cup honey (optional)
- 1 tsp vanilla extract
- 1 cup carrots (shredded)
- 1 tsp baking soda
- 1 large egg

Instructions:

To start, preheat oven to 350°F (175°C). Lightly grease a 6-cup ring mold or fluted tube pan.

In a large bowl, add egg, honey, peanut butter, oil & vanilla. Blend until well combined. Stir in shredded carrots and combine the mixture. Sift together flour & baking soda, then fold into carrot mixture until a smooth batter forms.

Spoon batter into prepared pan. Place pan into oven and bake for about 35 to 40 mins, or until a toothpick inserted comes out clean. Allow to cool in pan for about 10 mins, before transferring them to wire rack to cool completely.

Tips/Notes:

The addition of honey is totally optional, but makes the cake a sweeter treat for your dog (adjust sweetness according to your dog's taste preference).

You can substitute whole wheat flour with brown rice flour for a gluten-free alternative.

If peanut butter is a concern, consider using almond or sunflower seed butter.

Ingredients:
- 1 cup rice flour
- 1 cup carrot (grated)
- ½ cup rolled oats
- ½ cup applesauce
- 2 tsp cinnamon
- 2 large eggs

Icing
- ½ cup plain greek yogurt
- 2 ozs cream cheese

Instructions:
To start, preheat oven to 350°F (180°C). In a large bowl, combine eggs & applesauce. Mix together until well combined. Stir in carrots, then add in flour, rolled oats & cinnamon (if your mixture comes out too stiff, add a bit more applesauce or water). Spoon mixture into a muffin tin (cupcake liners optional but if you don't use them, grease the tin beforehand). Place into oven and bake for about 25 mins, or until pupcakes are firm. Allow to cool completely

For the Icing
In a small bowl, beat cream cheese until smooth. Gradually stir in yogurt until a consistent mixture is achieved. Spoon icing over cooled pupcakes, then serve to your dog.

Tips/Notes:
If your dig is lactose-intolerant, opt for lactose-free yogurt, same with cream cheese. This recipe makes about 8 pupcakes, yours may vary due to many reasons. Store pupcakes inside refrigerator in sealed container for up to 5 days, or in ziplock bag and freeze for up to 3 months without frosting.

Ingredients:

- 2 cups whole wheat flour
- ½ cup sweet potato (purée)
- ¾ lb ground turkey (cooked & drained)
- ⅓ plain greek yogurt
- 2 tsps baking powder
- ¼ cup coconut oil
- ¼ cup organic honey
- ⅔ cup frozen peas & carrots
- 1 large egg

Frosting

- 4 ozs cream cheese (at room temperature)
- ¼ cup sweet potato (purée)
- 1 tbsp organic honey

Instructions:

To start, preheat oven to 350°F (175°C). Lightly spray a 9-inch cake pan with nonstick cooking spray.

In a small bowl, whisk together flour & baking powder. In another but medium bowl, add sweet potato puree, yogurt, oil, honey, & egg. Whisk together until well combined.

Add dry ingredients to wet ingredients, mix until evenly moistened. Gently fold in cooked turkey, frozen peas & carrots. Spoon batter into prepared cake pan, then use an offset spatula to smooth the edges. Place into oven and bake for about 22 to 27 mins, or until a toothpick inserted in center comes out clean.

Allow cake to cool completely before frosting.

For The Frosting

In a small bowl, use an electric handheld mixer to beat cream cheese until light and fluffy. Add in sweet potato & honey, continue to beat until well combined.

Pipe or spread frosting onto cooled cake, then decorate as desired.

Tips/Notes:

You can customize the cake decorations based on your dog's preferences, such as using additional vegetables or dog-friendly treats.

Ingredients:

- 2 cups all-purpose flour
- ½ cup old-fashioned rolled oats
- 1 cup apple (shredded)
- 1 cup cheddar cheese (shredded)
- 2 tbsps organic honey
- 2 tsps baking powder
- 2 whole eggs
- ¾ cup plain greek yogurt
- ¼ cup vegetable (or canola oil)

Frosting

- 7 to 8 ozs cream cheese (room temperature)
- 2 tbsps organic honey
- 2 tbsps plain greek yogurt

Instructions:

To start, preheat oven to 350°F (175°C). Line a muffin tin with paper or silicone cupcake liners.

In a large bowl, add yogurt, oil, honey & eggs. Whisk together to combine. In another but medium bowl, whisk together flour, oats & baking powder until well combined.

Pour dry ingredients into wet ingredients bowl, mix until evenly moistened. Gently fold in shredded apples & cheddar until a smooth batter forms.

Evenly divide batter among cavities of your prepared pan, filling the cups to about ¾ full. Bake for about 16 to 20 mins, or until a toothpick inserted into center comes out clean.

Once done, remove cakes from muffin tin, allow to cool completely on a wire rack before frosting.

For The Frosting

In a bowl, beat together cream cheese, honey & yogurt until light and creamy, using an electric handheld mixer. Pipe or spread the frosting on top cooled pupcakes. Decorate as you wish before serving to your dog.

Tips/Notes:

You can also try this recipe using other dog-friendly cheeses like mozzarella or goat cheese.

If your dog has allergies, consider substituting flour with alternatives like coconut flour or oat flour.

Ingredients:
- 1¼ cups dog food
- ½ cup pumpkin puree
- 2½ tbsps natural peanut butter

Frosting
- 1 cup powdered sugar
- 2 tbsps sprinkles
- 2 tbsps water

Instructions:
In a food processor, put dog food, pumpkin puree & peanut butter. Pulse until mixture resembles coarse crumbs and sticks together. Press mixture into a 4-inch springform mini cake pan until a cake shape forms (Alternatively, you can roll it into a cake pop). Once done, remove formed cake from pan.

For The Frosting
In a bowl, mix powdered sugar with water, then pour mixture over top of your cake. Evenly spread it with a spatula, decorate with sprinkles to added flavor.

Tips/Notes:
You can use any dry dog food for this recipe or just your dog's favorites.

You can use a cupcake or cake pop mold for shaping; get creative and press it into a cookie cutter or roll it into a ball, then dip top in icing if you desire.

This recipe is also suitable for cats if you have one, simply switch dog food/treats with cat food/treats.

Ingredients:

- 1 cup duck (minced)
- 1 cup beef (minced)
- 1 tbsp coconut oil
- 5 to 6 dehydrated sprats
- Some berries (strawberry, blueberry etc)

Instructions:

To start, thaw minced meats and distribute them evenly into four cake tins or flat bowls, creating two layers of minced beef and two layers of minced duck.

Place tins in the freezer for about 3 hrs until layers are completely frozen. Once done, remove frozen layers from tins, then stack all four layers while alternating the types of meat. Now, drizzle melted coconut oil on top, allowing it to firm up quickly. Then add small drops of coconut oil, use it as adhesive to attach your berries. Drizzle some coconut oil on the sides and use it to stick the dehydrated sprats.

Serve the cake frozen, or allow it to thaw before serving if your dog prefer non-frozen treats.

Tips/Notes:

Use only dog-friendly coconut oil specifically formulated for dogs without harmful additives.

Your duck and beef meat should be about 225 grams each.

You will need some handful of berries/fruits (straw, blue, black or even diced apples) for this recipe.

Ingredients:

- 3 cups whole wheat flour
- 2 bananas (mashed)
- 2 tsp pure vanilla extract
- 2 whole eggs
- 1 tsp baking soda
- 1 cup applesauce (unsweetened)
- ¼ cup unsalted walnuts (chopped)
- ¼ cup honey
- ½ cup vegetable oil
- ½ cup sour cream

Frosting

- 1 tsp pure vanilla extract
- ¼ cup sour cream
- ¼ cup honey
- ½ cup vegetable oil

Instructions:

To start preheat oven to 350°F (175°C).

In a large bowl, combine all cake ingredients until a smooth batter forms. Pour batter into a greased and floured 9- by 13- by 2-inch baking pan.

Place pan into oven and bake for about 45 to 50 mins, or until cake is completely cooked and a toothpick inserted in the center comes out clean. Allow to cake to cool completely on a wire rack. Once cooled, prepare the frosting.

In a bowl, beat sour cream, vegetable oil, honey & vanilla until creamy. If the mixture is too soft, cover and refrigerate it until it thickens. Once thick, spread mixture evenly over the cake to frost it. Serve!

Tips/Notes:

If your frosting comes out too sweet, balance it by adding a bit more sour cream, or use greek yogurt for a tangy twist.

You can experiment with different fruit toppings like sliced strawberries or blueberries for added freshness.

Ingredients:

- ¾ cup solid-pack pumpkin
- ¾ cup whole wheat flour
- ¼ cup organic honey
- 2 or 3 whole eggs
- 1 tsp baking powder
- 1 tsp baking soda
- 1 tsp ground ginger
- 2 tsps ground cinnamon
- ½ tsp ground nutmeg
- ½ cup applesauce (unsweetened)

Filling

- 6 to 8 ozs cream cheese, softened
- 1 tsp pure vanilla extract
- 1 tsp honey
- ¼ cup vegetable oil

Instructions:

To start, preheat oven to 375°F (190°C). Line a 9- by 13-inch jelly-roll pan with wax paper.

In a large bowl, combine all cake ingredients until a smooth batter forms. Pour batter into prepared pan, then evenly spread it. Place pan into oven and bake for about 12 to 13 mins, or until a toothpick inserted in center comes out clean.

Once done, remove cake from pan and place onto a towel. Remove wax paper, and roll cake and towel together.

Allow cake to cool completely.

For the Filling

In a small bowl, blend cream cheese together with remaining filling ingredients. Once cake is cool, carefully unroll it and spread filling mixture evenly across cake.

Reroll the cake again, then serve.

Alternatively; If you find it hard rolling the cake, just cut it into equal portions. Thinly spread the filling between the slices, put one slice on top another until all slices are used up. Frost entire cake with filling.

Tips/Notes:

Be sure to choose low-fat cream cheese; while maple syrup can be used as a honey substitute.

You can substitute whole wheat flour with all-purpose flour, or try almond flour instead for a gluten-free version.

Ingredients:

- 1½ cup carrot (grated)
- 2 cups oat flour
- 2 medium ripe bananas (peeled)
- 2 whole eggs
- 3½ tbsps coconut oil (melted)
- 1 tsp baking soda
- 1 tsp baking powder
- 1 cup oat milk (unsweetened)
- ½ cup natural peanut butter
- 1 tbsp coconut oil

Frosting

- ½ cup greek yogurt non-fat
- ¼ cup natural peanut butter

Instructions:

To start, preheat oven to 350°F (175°C). Lightly grease cake silicone mold with coconut oil and set aside. In a large mixing bowl, add bananas, peanut butter & melted oil. Mix until well combined. Add in eggs and mix again to combine. Sift in oat flour, baking powder & baking soda until well combined. Gradually pour in oat milk while mixing, then fold in shredded carrot until a smooth batter forms. Pour into a 7x10-inch bone-shaped silicone cake pan.

Place pan into oven and bake for about 35 to 40 to mins, or until a toothpick inserted comes out clean. Allow cake to cool completely.

For the Frosting

Using a hand mixer, whip together yogurt & peanut butter until mixture is combined and fluffy. Once cake is completely cooled, cover with frosting and decorate with all-natural dog-friendly sprinkles or toppings of your choice!

Tips/Notes:

If you won't be using a stand-mixer, you will need to mash bananas first using a fork.

You can substitute oat flour with ground rolled oats; oat milk with whole milk if desired.

The frosting is totally optional, but you can include it if it's your dog's favorite part of the cake; also consider topping the pupcake with all-natural sprinkles or dog bones if desire.

Ingredients:

- 1 medium apple (shredded)
- 1 egg (beaten)
- ½ tsp baking powder
- 2½ tbsps applesauce (unsweetened)
- milk-bone biscuit (for decoration)

Instructions:

To start, preheat oven to 350°F (175°C). Lightly grease a small muffin tin, and set aside.

In a medium bowl, combine egg, applesauce, apple & baking powder. Mix until well combined and a smooth batter forms.

Pour batter into muffin tins and top each pupcakes with milk-bone mini biscuits for decoration. Place into oven and bake pupcakes for about 35 to 40 mins, or until toothpick inserted comes out clean & tops are browned. Allow to cool before serving to your dog.

Tips/Notes:

Your batter should be able to yield about 5 regular-sized muffins. This pupcakes recipe is perfect to show your pup some love on valentine's day.

Ingredients:

- 1 lb ground beef
- 2 tbsps flour
- 1½ cups potatoes (cooked & mashed)
- ½ cup cheese (shredded or crumbled)
- 1 cup beef broth (low sodium)
- 1 large egg (beaten)
- 1 tbsp tomato paste
- ½ cup corn
- ½ cup peas
- ½ cup plain breadcrumbs

Instructions:

To start, preheat oven to 400°F. Spray a pie dish with nonstick cooking spray. In a large skillet or pan, cook ground beef over medium-high heat until browned. Drain any excess fat. Sprinkle flour over cooked beef, then toss to coat, continue cooking for an additional minute.

Add tomato paste & beef broth, stir to combine. Bring to a boil, then reduce heat to low, cover and simmer for about 5 mins, or until sauce slightly thickens. Add in corn, peas, breadcrumbs & beaten egg; mix until well combined. Spread mixture evenly into prepared pie dish.

In a large bowl, combine potatoes & cheese. Pipe or spoon mixture on top meat mixture. Then place pie dish on baking sheet. Bake for about 20 mins, or until potatoes start to brown. Once done, transfer pie to a cooling rack, allow to cool completely before serving.

Tips/Notes:

If your dog is lactose intolerant, just omit milk & butter in this recipe, your dog will still love the taste.

Ingredients:
- 1½ cup whole wheat flour
- ½ cup sweet potato puree (baby food)
- ¾ lb ground turkey (cooked & drained)
- 2 tsps baking powder
- 1 large egg
- ¼ cup plain greek yogurt
- ¼ cup coconut oil
- ¼ cup organic honey
- ⅔ cup frozen peas & carrots

Frosting
- 4 ozs cream cheese (at room temperature)
- ¼ cup sweet potato puree
- 1 tbsp organic honey

Instructions:
To start, preheat oven to 350°F (175°C). Spray a 9-inch cake pan with nonstick cooking spray. In a small bowl, add flour & baking powder. Mix together to combine.

In a medium bowl, combine sweet potato puree, honey, yogurt, oil & egg. Whisk until combined. Add dry ingredients to wet ingredients, mix until evenly moistened.

Gently fold in cooked turkey, peas & carrots, mix until a smooth batter forms. Spoon batter into prepared cake pan, then use an offset spatula to smooth edges.

Bake for about 25 to 30 mins, or until a toothpick inserted into center comes out clean. Allow to cool completely before frosting.

<u>For The Frosting</u>

In a small bowl, beat cream cheese with an electric handheld mixer until light & fluffy.

Add in sweet potato & honey. Continue to beat until well combined. Pipe or spread mixture onto cooled cake and decorate as desired.

Tips/Notes:

You can experiment with different dog-friendly decorations for a personalized touch.

Store the cake in the refrigerator if not consumed immediately, and serve in moderation.

Ingredients:
- 1½ cups whole wheat flour
- 1½ cups oat flour
- 1 cup applesauce (unsweetened)
- 1 cup apples (finely chopped)
- 1 large egg
- 1 tsp baking powder
- 2 tbsps honey
- ¼ tsp cinnamon

Instructions:
To start, preheat oven to 350°F (175°C).

In a medium bowl, combine applesauce, egg & honey together with a whisk. Leave apples behind.

In another bowl, combine all dry ingredients (flours, baking powder & cinnamon). Stir dry mixture into wet ingredient bowl. Mix until well combined. Fold in chopped apple pieces. Spoon batter into mini muffin tins/pans, about ¾ of the way full. Bake for about 25 to 30mins, or until a toothpick inserted comes out clean. Allow to cool before serving.

Tips/Notes:
This recipe doesn't require paper liners otherwise pupcakes will stick to liners. Just grease your muffin pan or tin with butter or oil instead.

If you have a pet with grain allergy, try swapping out the wheat flour for coconut or almond flour instead.

Ingredients:

- 1 cup apples (chopped)
- 1 tbsp baking powder
- 1 large egg
- 4 tbsps honey
- 4 cups whole wheat flour
- ¼ cups apple sauce
- ¼ tsp vanilla extract
- 5½ ozs vanilla candiquik
- 2 cups water (adjust)

Instructions:

To start, preheat oven to 350°F (175°C).

In a large bowl, mix water, applesauce, vanilla, egg & honey. Whisk together to mix. Combine whole wheat flour & baking powder. Stir into wet ingredients.

Next, fold in chopped apples. Then spoon the mixture into greased muffin tins. Bake for about 35 mins, or until golden brown. Then allow to cool.

Melt candiquik according to package directions. Pour it into a piping bag (or plastic bag with one corner snipped off). Pipe on designs.

Tips/Notes:

If you've got a donut pan, you can also make treats into bagel or fun donut shapes. But if I have a bone-shaped cupcake pan, that's great.

This recipe takes about 50 mins to an hour, to get prep and cook.

Ingredients:

- ½ lb ground beef
- 1 cup old-fashioned rolled oats
- 1 cup mixed vegetables (diced)
- 1 lb ground turkey
- 2 large eggs
- ¼ cup fresh parsley (chopped)

For Frosting

- 3 large sweet potatoes
- 8 ozs cream cheese

Instructions:

To start, preheat oven to 350° F (175°C). Grease three 6-inch cake pans with non-stick spray or coconut oil.

In a large bowl, add turkey, beef, eggs, oats, veggies & parsley. Mix until well combined. Divide meat mixture evenly between the three pans. Bake for about 25 to 30 mins, or until layers turn golden brown.

Remove baked layers from oven, allow to cool completely in the pans on top wire rack.

For Frosting

Allow cream cheese soften to room temperature. Then peel and dice sweet potatoes. Bring a large pot of water to a boil. Add sweet potatoes to and boil until tender.

Drain sweet potatoes, allow them to cool completely. Do not make the frosting with hot or warm sweet potatoes.

Using a mixer or potato masher, combine cream cheese & sweet potatoes. Mix until evenly smooth.

Once cooled, remove one cake layer from the pan and place it on a serving plate or cake stand. Frost top of the layer. Add another layer and frost the top again. Add third layer and frost the top and sides of the cake.

For Topping

In a plastic zip-top bag, place dog biscuits and seal the bag. Use a rolling pin, roll over bag and crush the biscuits into small pieces.

Sprinkle dog biscuit pieces on the top of the cake. Slice and serve to your pooch.

Tips/Notes:

Veggies like peas, carrots, zucchini, green beans, broccoli & cauliflower are great choices too. Adding dog biscuits toppings is totally optional.

Ingredients:

- ⅔ cup strawberries (mashed)
- ¼ cup refined coconut oil
- 1 cup almond milk (unsweetened)
- 2½ cups chickpea flour
- 2 tsps lemon juice
- 1 tsp baking powder
- 1 tsp baking soda
- 1 tsp cinnamon

Frosting

- 1 cup plain greek or dairy-free yogurt
- 1 tbsp maple syrup

Instructions:

To start, preheat oven to 350°F (175°C). Line a small cake pan with parchment paper.

In a small bowl, sift together chickpea flour, cinnamon, baking powder & baking soda (dry ingredients).

In a separate bowl, whisk together almond milk, coconut oil & lemon juice (wet ingredients).

Combine wet and dry ingredients in one mixing bowl. Mix in about ½ cup mashed strawberries until a smooth batter forms. Pour batter into cake pan and place in the oven.

Bake for about 30 to 35 mins, or until a toothpick inserted in center comes out clean. Once done, allow cake to cool, then place it in freezer for about 30 mins.

For The Frosting

In a bowl, whip dairy-free yogurt & maple syrup. Cut cake from center (half horizontally) to make two tiers. Spread about ½ cup dairy-free yogurt among each tier of cake, and gently stack cakes on top of each other. Decorate top with leftover frosting and remaining mashed strawberries.

Tips/Notes:

You'll need to reserve about half or less of the mashed strawberries for garnishing.

If chickpea flour is unavailable, you can try using oat flour or a gluten-free all-purpose flour.

Ingredients:

- 1 apple (finely grated)
- ½ cup sweet potato (purée)
- ½ cup whole wheat flour
- ½ cup applesauce (unsweetened)
- 2 tbsps rolled oats (not quick)
- 1 tbsp honey
- 1 tbsp coconut oil
- 1 egg (beaten)

Icing
- 2 ozs cream cheese
- 2 tbsps applesauce (unsweetened)

Instructions:

To start, preheat oven to 350°F (175°C). Lightly grease a cupcake pan with nonstick cooking spray.

In a large bowl, combine sweet potato puree, apple, applesauce, honey & coconut oil. Pour in beaten egg, stir until well incorporated, add in flour & uncooked oats into the mixture. Continue to stir until dough comes together. Slowly dollop batter in on your greased lined cupcake pans (don't worry if yours come out too thick, just continue).

Place into oven and bake for about 15 to 30 mins, or until toothpick inserted comes out clean. Once done, allow pupcakes to cool.

In another bowl, combine cream cheese & applesauce. Beat together with a hand mixer and set aside until needed.

Once cakes are cooled, top it with icing before serving to your dog.

Tips/Notes:
For a grain-free alternative, substitute whole wheat flour with almond flour or keep it paleo by using coconut flour.
For a lighter texture, try baking the pupcakes in mini cupcake pans; you can then easily cut them in half before serving to ensure your dog can comfortably enjoy them.

Ingredients:
- 2 cups applesauce (unsweetened)
- 2½ cups whole wheat flour
- 1½ tsp baking soda
- ½ tsp baking powder
- ½ cup vegetable oil
- ⅓ cup honey
- 2 whole eggs
- 1 tsp ground cinnamon
- ½ tsp allspice

Frosting
- 6 to 8 ozs cream cheese (softened)
- ⅓ cup vegetable oil
- 1 tsp pure vanilla extract

Instructions:
To start preheat oven to 350°F (175°C).

In a large bowl, mix all cake ingredients until a smooth batter forms. Pour batter into a greased and floured 9 X 13 X 2 inch baking pan. Bake inside oven for about 45 to 50 mins, or until cake is completely cooked and a toothpick inserted in the center comes out clean. Allow to cake to cool completely on a wire rack. Once cooled, prepare the frosting. In a bowl, beat cream cheese, vegetable oil & vanilla until creamy. Spread the frosting evenly over cake to frost it. The serve!

Tips/Notes:
Be sure applesauce is at room temperature to prevent it from solidifying the vegetable oil.

For a lighter version of this recipe, use low-fat cream cheese in the frosting.

Ingredients:
- 1½ cups whole wheat flour
- 1 cup quick-cooking oats (uncooked)
- ½ cup unsalted walnuts (chopped)
- ¼ cup organic honey
- ¼ cup vegetable oil
- 2 whole eggs
- ½ tsp ground nutmeg
- 1 tsp ground cinnamon
- 1 tsp pure vanilla extract

Frosting
- 6 to 8 ozs cream cheese (softened)
- ⅓ cup vegetable oil
- 2 tsps orange rind (grated)

Instructions:
To start preheat oven to 350°F (175°C).
In a large bowl, mix all cake ingredients until a smooth batter forms. Pour batter into a greased and floured 8 X 16 X 2 inch baking pan. Bake for about 35 to 45 mins, or until cake is completely cooked and a toothpick inserted in the center comes out clean. Allow to cake to cool completely on a wire rack. Once cooled, prepare the frosting. In a bowl, beat cream cheese & vegetable oil until creamy. Gradually beat in orange rind. Spread frosting evenly over cake to frost it.
Then serve!

Tips/Notes:
You can decorate frosted cake with additional chopped walnuts or a sprinkle of cinnamon for visual appeal.
You can also try the recipe with different citrus fruits like lemon or lime for a unique twist to the frosting.

Ingredients:
- 1 cup whole wheat flour
- ½ cup pumpkin puree
- ½ cup applesauce (unsweetened)
- ⅛ cup vegetable oil
- ¼ cup natural peanut butter
- ½ tsp baking soda
- 1 large egg

Frosting (Optional)
- ½ cup plain greek yogurt
- ¼ cup natural peanut butter

Instructions:
To start, preheat oven to 350°F (175°C). Lightly grease an 6 or 8-inch round pan or square pan with oil.

In a large bowl, combine flour & baking soda until well mixed. In another bowl, mix together vegetable oil, peanut butter, applesauce & pumpkin puree. Next, add in egg, then continue to mix until well combined. Combine wet and dry ingredients using a rubber spatula, stir until combined.

Pour mixture into your greased pan, then place into oven. Bake for about 25 to 30 mins, or until cake springs back when pressed lightly. Allow to cool on a wire rack before removing it from pan. Once cooled, prepare the frosting. In a stand mixer or bowl, beat yogurt & peanut butter until light & fluffy. Spread a thin layer of frosting over cake.

Serve immediately.

Tips/Notes:
This recipe yields about one 8" round cake, and you can double it to make a layer cake; should be store in the fridge.

Ingredients:

For Cookie

- 1½ cups whole wheat flour
- 1 cup oatmeal
- 1 large egg
- 1 carrot (shredded)
- ½ apple (peeled & shredded)
- ¾ cup water

For Frosting

- 1 cup plain greek yogurt (or vanilla)
- 2 tbsps peanut butter

Instructions:

To start, preheat oven to 400° F (200°C).

In a large bowl, mix all cookie ingredients together until they form a ball. Roll out dough on a floured surface about ¼ inch thickness. Using a heart-shaped cookie cutter, cut out cookies. Using your finger, press down shape of a paw print in the center of each cookie. Press firmly to ensure the shape remains after cooking. Place cookies on a greased baking sheet, bake for about 20 mins. Allow to cool completely.

Once cooled, prepare the frosting. In a bowl, mix yogurt & peanut butter until smooth. Once cookies are completely cooled, fill each paw print shape with frosting. Store in an airtight container in fridge for up to 1 week, or until yogurt expires.

Tips/Notes:

You can use a butter knife or your finger to fill the paw prints.

Ingredients:

- 1½ cups whole wheat flour
- 1½ cups old-fashioned oats
- 1 cup peanut butter
- 2 whole eggs
- ½ cup applesauce (unsweetened)

For Frosting

- 1 cup plain greek yogurt
- ½ cup bacon bits (optional)

Instructions:

In a large bowl combine peanut butter, applesauce & eggs. Whisk until smooth. Add in flour & oats. Mix well until it forms a stiff dough.

Roll out dough to about ½ inch thick circle. Using a well-floured doughnut cutter, cut out desired number of donuts, (re-roll and repeat until all dough is used up). Place donuts in air fryer basket in a single layer. Preheat air fry and cook at 340°F (171°C) for about 10 mins. Let it rest in basket for an additional 5 mins, before removing them.

Allow donuts to cool completely before frosting them.

For The Frosting

Spread a thick layer of greek yogurt (about 2 tbsps) on top cooled donuts.

If desired, sprinkle a tablespoon of bacon bits on the donuts. Then serve!

Tips/Notes:

You can always get creative with ingredients, long as they are safe for your dog.

Store any leftover donuts in an airtight container in the refrigerator for up to a week, or pop base in the freezer for later.

This recipe should be able to yields about 8 donuts using a 3.5-inches cutter.

Ingredients:

- 2 cups unbleached white flour
- 1 cup low-fat plain yogurt
- 1 cup applesauce (unsweetened)
- ½ cup unsalted walnuts (chopped)
- ⅓ cup organic honey
- 1½ tsps baking powder
- ½ tsp baking soda
- ½ tsp ground cinnamon
- 2 whole eggs

Instructions:

To start preheat oven to 350°F (175°C).

In a large bowl, mix all cake ingredients until a smooth batter forms. Pour batter into a greased and floured 9 X 13 X 2 inch baking pan. Bake inside oven for about 30 to 35

Mins, or until cake is completely cooked and a toothpick inserted in the center comes out clean. Allow cake to cool completely on a wire rack.

Once done, remove and serve to your dog.

Ingredients:

- 2 cups unbleached white flour
- ½ cup wheat germ
- ½ cup applesauce (unsweetened)
- ¼ cup organic honey
- 4 ozs cream cheese (softened)
- ½ tsp baking soda
- 1 tsp pure vanilla extract
- 2 tsp baking powder
- 2 whole eggs
- ½ cup water

Instructions:

To start preheat oven to 350ºF (175°C).

In a medium bowl, combine and mix all wet ingredients. In a large bowl, mix all dry ingredients. Gradually pour wet ingredients into dry mixture. Mix togeth until a smooth batter forms. Pour into a greased 9- by 13-inch baking pan. Place pan into oven and bake for about 40 to 45 mins, until cake is completely cooked and a toothpick inserted in the center comes out clean. Allow cake to cool completely on a wire rack. Once done, remove and serve to your dog.

Ingredients:

- 2½ cups oat flour
- ½ tsp baking soda
- ½ cup applesauce (unsweetened)
- 2 tbsps coconut oil (melted)
- 1 medium apple (finely chopped)
- 1 medium banana (mashed)
- 1 large egg
- water (adjust as needed)

For Icing

- ½ cup plain greek yogurt
- ½ cup natural peanut butter

Instructions:

In a medium bowl, add oat flour & baking soda. Mix together until well combined. In another bowl, combine egg, applesauce, banana, apple & melted oil. Whisk together until smooth. Add wet ingredients into dry ingredients mixture. Mix until well combined (if dough comes out a little dry, add a small amount of water, then continue mixing).

Place batter into a silicone mold that fits in your air fryer.

Air fryer at 325°F for about 12 to 15 mins. Then transfer fries to a wire rack to cool to room temperature.

For The Icing

In a bowl, combine greek yogurt & peanut butter. Then spread icing on top treats. Alternatively, simply frost treats with peanut butter & greek yogurt. Or crumble a treat, then use it as topping.

69

Tips/Notes:

If you don't have oat flour, make one by blending 2 cups of uncooked old-fashioned oat in a blender until smooth flour.

You can also cut out treats using your favorite-shaped cookie-cutter.

Remember to store treats in an airtight container in fridge especial those yogurt icing, while those with only peanut butter icing can be stored at room temperature.

CONCLUSION

Now that you know how to make a safe and delicious dog-friendly cakes for your canine companion, it's time to get the celebrations started.

The recipes in **"DOG BIRTHDAY COOKBOOK"** are all-natural, affordable, delicious and equally easy-to-follow. There are many variations of these air frying recipes that you can make, but before feeding to your dog, I highly recommend you consult with your vet beforehand.

I hope you found a few recipes that cut your attention and that of your dog. If yes, continue to explore the vibrant flavors within this cookbook. Let it be your companion in your quest to healthier and happy life for your dog.

Your feedback is invaluable, and so I wholeheartedly extend a sincere invitation to share an honest review about this dog cake cookbook.

Until then, happy birthday to your pup!

Your Friend,
Scott Thelton

for choosing
this cookbook

BONUS

"SLOW COOKER DOG FOOD COOOKBOOK"

SCAN TO
DOWNLOAD
YOUR FREE
BONUS BOOK

Printed in Great Britain
by Amazon

43345992R00046